curious
NATURE

HUMAN BODY

QUESTIONS & ANSWERS

NANCY DICKMANN

W

FRANKLIN WATTS
LONDON • SYDNEY

Published in paperback in 2017 by
The Watts Publishing Group

For Brown Bear Books Ltd:
Text and Editor: Nancy Dickmann
Editorial Director: Lindsey Lowe
Children's Publisher: Anne O'Daly
Design Manager: Keith Davis
Designer and Illustrator: Supriya Sahai
Picture Manager: Sophie Mortimer

Concept development: Square and Circus/Brown Bear
Books Ltd

ISBN: 978 1 4451 5677 4

Printed in Malaysia

Franklin Watts
An imprint of
Hachette Children's Group
Part of the Watts Publishing Group
Carmelite House
50 Victoria Embankment
London EC4Y 0DZ

An Hachette UK company
www.hachette.co.uk
www.franklinwatts.co.uk

Picture Credits
All photographs copyright Shutterstock except
page 10 Thinkstock and page 19 NOAA Photo Library.

Brown Bear Books has made every attempt to
contact the copyright holder. If you have any information
please contact licensing@brownbearbooks.co.uk

Websites
The website addresses (URLs) included in this book
were valid at the time of going to press. However,
it is possible that contents or addresses may change
following the publication of this book. No responsibility
for any such changes can be accepted by either the
author or the publisher.

CONTENTS

HOW DOES MY BODY WORK?

Your body is amazing. It can walk, run and dance. Your body can whisper, shout and sing. It can turn food into energy. It can think and remember. It even knows exactly how to grow and develop.

All of these things are controlled by one incredible organ: your brain! Your brain is like a powerful computer. It takes in messages from body parts, such as your eyes or ears. Then it tells the body what to do.

Brain

PARTS OF THE BODY

Your body is made of tiny building blocks called cells. Groups of similar cells join together. They form tissues. Some tissues join together to make organs. Your heart, lungs and stomach are all organs.

THINK ABOUT IT

Sometimes, you decide what your body does. You decide to use your hand to pick up a book. But you don't have to tell your heart to beat or your lungs to breathe. Your brain controls these things without you thinking about them. It even works when you are asleep!

WHAT IS A NERVE?

Your brain doesn't do everything by itself. It is connected to the spinal cord. This cord runs down your back. Nerve cells are a special type of cell. Bundles of them come out of the spinal cord. They form a network that goes through your whole body.

The nerves act like wires that carry electricity. They take messages from the brain to the rest of your body. They also take messages from your body back to your brain.

INSTANT MESSAGES

Nerves send messages very quickly. The signals can travel at 386 kilometres per hour. That's faster than a racing car!

Nerve cell

Nerves in your fingers send messages about things that you touch.

SENDING A MESSAGE

1. Your teacher asks you to stand up. The sound travels across the room.

3. Your brain receives the message. It decides what to do. Then it sends out a message.

2. Your ears take in the sound. They send a message to your brain.

4. Nerves carry the message to your leg muscles. The muscles pull on your bones to make you stand up.

HOW MANY BONES DO I HAVE?

That depends on how old you are! A baby has about 300 bones when it is born. Some of these bones fuse together as the baby grows. An adult has only 206 bones. More than half are in the hands and feet.

Your bones make up your skeleton. The skeleton's job is to hold the body up. Without it, you would be too floppy to stand!

If a bone breaks, it can take a while to heal.

JOINTS

Bones are hard and cannot bend. Your body can only bend at places where bones join together. These places are called joints. Elbows, hips, shoulders, knees and ankles are joints. Tough, stretchy ligaments hold the bones together.

AMAZING BONES

Your **skull** has 21 bones that are fused together. The jawbone makes 22!

Your body has 12 pairs of **ribs**.

The **femur** is your thigh bone. It is the longest bone in the body.

Many muscles attach to your **pelvis.** They let you walk, run and sit.

Your kneecap is called the **patella.**

Your **ankles** are made of lots of small bones.

9

HOW DO MUSCLES WORK?

Bones can't move by themselves. Your body needs muscles to move. You have more than 600 muscles. Some are big and others are tiny. Many muscles are attached to bones.

Muscles are made of many thin fibres. They are stretchy, like a rubber band. When a muscle contracts, or gets shorter, it pulls on the bone. This makes the bone move.

A simple smile takes a lot of muscles working together!

SMOOTH MUSCLES
The walls of your stomach are made of smooth muscles. These muscles are not attached to bones. They squeeze to break up food inside the stomach. Other smooth muscles push blood around your body.

HOW MUSCLES MOVE BONES

Muscles can pull, but they can't push. Many muscles work
in pairs. One muscle raises your arm.
Another muscle lowers it.

Raising your arm
The **biceps** muscle contracts.
It pulls on the bone in your lower arm.
This raises your lower arm.

biceps
muscle

Lowering your arm
The biceps can't push your
arm back down. Instead, the
triceps muscle contracts. It
pulls your lower arm down.

triceps
muscle

WHY CAN'T I SEE IN THE DARK?

You see things when light enters your eyes. Special cells inside your eye receive the light. They send a message to the brain. The brain turns these signals into the picture that you see. If it is very dark, there is no light to enter your eyes.

Seeing is one of your five senses. Your senses send messages about the world to your brain.

BROWS AND LASHES

Eyes are delicate, so they must be protected. Eyebrows keep sweat or rain from dripping into your eyes. Eyelashes keep out dust and sand.

THE FIVE SENSES

Your **eyes** take in light. They send a message to your brain.

Sounds travel through air as invisible waves. Your **ears** pick up these waves. They send a message to the brain.

Brain

Your **tongue** gets information about the food you eat. It tells your brain what it tastes like.

Your **nose** takes in chemicals from the air. It tells your brain about them.

Your **skin** takes in information when you touch something. It tells your brain what it feels like.

Your tongue can tell if food is meaty, sweet, salty, bitter or sour.

13

WHY DOES MY STOMACH RUMBLE?

The food you eat goes through the stomach and intestines. These organs are part of your digestive system. Muscles squeeze to keep the food moving. They also help to break it up.

Gases travel through this system, too. When they get squeezed, it makes noise. It sounds like your stomach is growling.

The inside walls of the small intestine look like tiny fingers.

BURPING

Gas gets into your digestive system. Some comes in through your mouth. It is also produced when your food is broken down. Your body needs to get rid of the extra gas. Some of it comes out when you burp.

14

THE DIGESTIVE SYSTEM

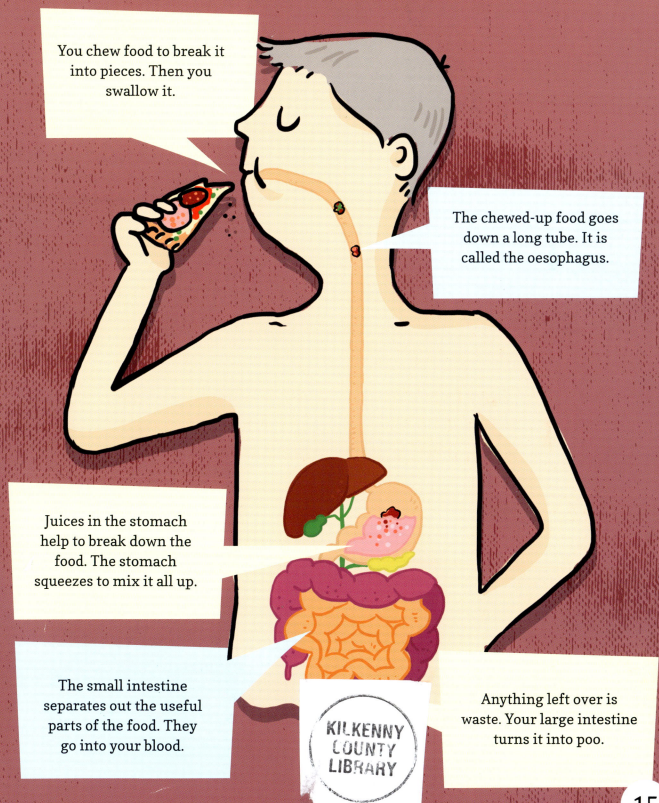

You chew food to break it into pieces. Then you swallow it.

The chewed-up food goes down a long tube. It is called the oesophagus.

Juices in the stomach help to break down the food. The stomach squeezes to mix it all up.

The small intestine separates out the useful parts of the food. They go into your blood.

Anything left over is waste. Your large intestine turns it into poo.

15

HOW DO I BREATHE?

Humans must breathe to live. Your body needs a gas called oxygen. It is found in the air. Your body uses it to release energy.

You breathe in oxygen through your mouth and nose. It goes down a tube and into your lungs. Your lungs are a bit like balloons. They expand when air goes into them. When the air goes out, they get smaller.

You breathe harder when you are active. This gives your body more oxygen.

HOW BREATHING WORKS

You breathe in air through your **mouth** and **nose**.

The air goes down the **tube**.

You breathe out air and **waste products**.

The tube splits into two parts. One goes into each **lung**.

The tubes split into smaller and smaller **branches**.

There is a **sheet of muscle** below your lungs. It flattens to pull air into your body.

There is a tiny sac at the end of each branch. The sacs are called **alveoli**. They let oxygen from the air move into your blood.

AMAZING ALVEOLI
You have at least 300 million alveoli in your lungs. If they were spread out, they would cover an area as big as a tennis court!

17

WHAT HAPPENS WHEN MY HEART BEATS?

Put your hand on your chest. Can you feel your heart beating? Its steady rhythm keeps you alive. With each beat, your heart pumps blood around your body. The blood carries oxygen and other things that your cells need.

Blood flows through a network of tubes. They are called blood vessels. Your heart, lungs and blood vessels work together. They make sure that all your body parts get the supplies they need.

HOW MANY HEARTS?
Most animals have one heart. But a few animals have more. Octopuses and squid have three hearts. Earthworms have five!

INSIDE A HEART

3. When blood comes back from the lungs, it is rich in **oxygen**.

4. This time the other lower chamber squeezes. Blood pumps out of the heart. It goes to **all parts** of the body.

1. Blood comes into one of the heart's four **chambers**.

2. The lower chamber squeezes. It pushes the blood out through a blood vessel. It will travel to the **lungs**.

A blue whale's heart is as big as a car.

WHAT ARE SCABS MADE OF?

Your blood contains tiny cells called platelets. If you cut yourself, you bleed. Platelets help your blood to clot. They stick together at the cut to make a plug. A web of thin threads holds them together.

When the clot dries, it forms a scab. The scab protects the cut skin. It keeps germs and dirt out. The skin starts to heal. Eventually the scab falls off and you see the new skin underneath.

A scab forms after you cut your skin.

Platelets are tiny and odd-shaped. They stick together to help blood to clot.

WHAT BLOOD IS MADE OF

Plasma makes up more than half of your blood. Red blood cells are the other main ingredient. Platelets and white blood cells make up less than 1% of your blood.

Each part of your blood has a job to do.

Plasma is the liquid part of blood. It helps blood cells to move through your body.

Red blood cells carry oxygen to all parts of the body. They are shaped a bit like doughnuts.

White blood cells stop you from getting sick. They find germs and destroy them.

21

WHY DO I SWEAT?

You sweat when you are hot. Sweating helps your body to cool down. When you sweat, tiny glands in your skin release liquid. It is mostly made of water.

Once the sweat is on your skin, it evaporates. This means it turns into a gas. When it does this, it takes heat away from your body. You stop sweating once your body gets back to the right temperature.

SALTY SWEAT

Sweat also helps your body to get rid of waste. Salts and other waste products are in your sweat. They get left behind on your skin when the sweat evaporates. That's why your sweat tastes salty.

Skin sweats to help your body to control its **temperature**.

22

Your skin does a lot of important jobs.

Skin can **feel** heat, cold, pressure and pain. It can feel if things are rough or smooth. It sends this information to the brain.

Skin is **waterproof**. It stops our bodies from losing too much water. It stops water from getting in.

Skin **protects** our bodies. It acts like armour to keep out germs and dirt.

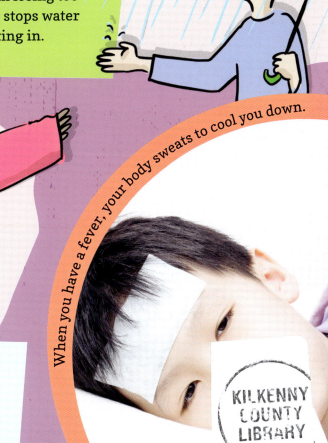

When you have a fever, your body sweats to cool you down.

23

HOW DOES MY BODY FIGHT GERMS?

Germs are tiny living things. Sometimes they get inside your body. Then they make copies of themselves. Germs can make you ill.

Luckily, your body is good at fighting them! White blood cells are one of the main weapons. They are made inside your bones. They attack and kill germs.

When you cough or sneeze, you can pass on germs.

24

ALLERGIES

Sometimes your body reacts to something harmless. This is called an allergy. Some people are allergic to pollen. When they breathe it in, their body treats it like a germ. It tries to fight it.

A few germs might get past your defences. If they do, you may get ill.

FIGHTING GERMS

Germs can enter through your mouth or nose. They can get in through a cut in your skin.

Small lumps filter out germs. They are called **lymph nodes.**

Sticky **mucus** inside your nose traps some germs.

White blood cells attack any germs that get in.

WHAT ARE HORMONES?

Your body doesn't just use nerves to communicate. Chemicals called hormones are another type of message. They keep your body working in the right way.

Hormones tell your heart to beat faster. They tell your bones to grow. They tell your muscles to shiver to warm you up. Body parts called glands make hormones. Your blood takes hormones where they need to go.

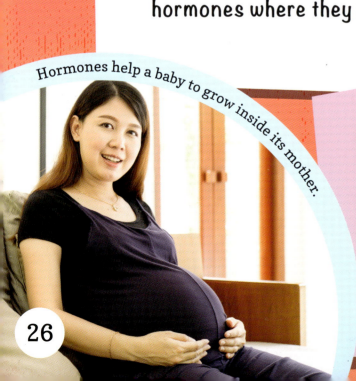
Hormones help a baby to grow inside its mother.

DIABETES
The right hormones will keep you healthy. A hormone called insulin controls the sugar in your blood. Too much sugar makes you ill. A person with diabetes doesn't make enough insulin.

Each hormone has a job to do.

Two hormones control how much sugar is in your blood.

Some hormones control how fast your cells work.

Growth hormones tell your body how and when to grow.

A hormone tells your body when to sleep. It tells it when to wake up.

One hormone helps you to react to danger. It makes your heart beat faster. It makes your body produce energy so you can run away.

Grrrrr

27

MAKE A STETHOSCOPE

 Your heart's steady beat keeps you alive. A doctor uses a stethoscope to listen to your heart. It is easy to make your own simple stethoscope. Then try it on your friends!

WHAT YOU NEED

* cardboard tube (from a roll of kitchen paper)
* funnel
* duct tape
* watch with a second hand or stopwatch

1 Put the funnel into one end of the cardboard tube.

2 Use duct tape to tape them together. Make sure you get a tight seal.

3 Put the funnel end on a friend's chest. Put your ear to the other end. Can you hear the heart beating?

4 Use a watch to time the heartbeat. How many beats can you count in 30 seconds?

A doctor listens to your body to find out if anything is wrong.

5 Ask your friend to do some jumping jacks, or run around for a while.

6 Listen to the heart and time it again. Is it beating faster than before?

TRY IT OUT

Try using your stethoscope on other body parts. Put the funnel on your friend's back. You can listen to their lungs as they breathe. You can also put it on their tummy. You might hear their stomach gurgling and growling.

GLOSSARY

cell tiny unit of life. Cells are the building blocks of the human body.

contract shrink or get smaller

digestive system group of organs that help your body to break down food and separate out the useful nutrients

energy ability to do work

evaporate turn from a liquid into a gas

expand get bigger or swell up

gland body part that makes liquids, such as hormones, sweat or tears

intestine long, coiled tube inside your body. Food passes through the intestines as it travels through the digestive system.

ligament band of tough tissue that connects bones to each other

lung sac-like organ in the chest. Lungs absorb oxygen from the air.

lymph node small lump of tissue that helps to filter out harmful substances. Lymph nodes are found in the armpits, neck and other places.

muscle bundle of fibres that can tighten or relax to move bones and other body parts

nerve fibre that carries messages to and from the brain

organ a body part that performs a particular task. The heart, brain, eyes and lungs are all organs.

oxygen gas found in the air that living things need to survive

platelet small particle found in the blood. Platelets help blood to clot.

sense one of the five ways that the body learns about its surroundings

FURTHER RESOURCES

BOOKS

First Encyclopedia of the Human Body,
Fiona Chandler (Usborne, 2011).

Human Body (Make Science Make Sense),
Anna Claybourne (Wayland, 2016).

Human Body: A Children's Encyclopedia
(Dorling Kindersley, 2012).

Utterly Amazing Human Body, Robert Winston
(Dorling Kindersley, 2015).

WEBSITES

www.bbc.co.uk/education/topics/zcyycdm
BBC Bitesize Key Stage 2 science, with short video clips
about the human body, from organs, muscles and bones
to the senses and digestion.

easyscienceforkids.com/human-body
Easy Science for Kids pages with lots of information and
fun facts about different parts of the human body.

**www.ngkids.co.uk/science-and-nature/15-facts-
about-the-human-body**
National Geographic Kids has 15 fascinating facts about
the human body, with links to pages on the digestive
system, the brain and eyes.

INDEX